REAL WORLD ECONOMICS™

How Commodities Trading Works

Laura La Bella

ROSEN
PUBLISHING®
New York

Published in 2011 by The Rosen Publishing Group, Inc.
29 East 21st Street, New York, NY 10010

Library of Congress Cataloging-in-Publication Data

La Bella, Laura.
How commodities trading works / Laura La Bella.
    p. cm.—(Real world economics)
Includes bibliographical references and index.
ISBN 978-1-4488-1273-8 (library binding)
1. Commodity exchanges—Juvenile literature. 2. Commodity exchanges—United States—Juvenile literature. I. Title.
HG6046.L2 2011
332.64'4—dc22

                                                                    2010013335

Manufactured in the United States of America

CPSIA Compliance Information: Batch #W11YA: For further information, contact Rosen Publishing, New York, New York, at 1-800-237-9932.

On the cover: Pit traders signal their desire to buy and sell crude oil, a major commodity, on the floor of the New York Mercantile Exchange.

Contents

INTRODUCTION

For thirteen straight days in January 2010, Florida was hit with severe, record-breaking cold temperatures. For a state that is the second largest producer of oranges in the world, a dramatic change in weather can be devastating to the fruit crop. To grow properly, the fruit requires warm temperatures and ample sunshine. After nearly two weeks of freezing weather, much of Florida's orange crop was devastated. It was estimated that nearly 30 percent of the crop was destroyed by the frigid weather. This loss meant two things. First, with the supply of oranges lower than the demand in 2010, the price of oranges would rise sharply. Second, that price hike would find its way to the consumer at the grocery store, impacting the family's grocery bill.

Oranges are just one of thousands of commodities that are traded every day. A commodity is a product or good that is uniform in quality and can be bought in large quantities.

Commodities can range from agricultural products, like oranges, corn, wheat, and livestock, to things that are more precious or nonrenewable, like metals and carbon-based energy (coal, oil). Commodities are in demand, have value, and are made by many different producers. Commodities are traded on a commodities market, where buyers and sellers come together to trade goods.

Commodities trading dates back more than six thousand years, when individuals and communities traded what they had for what they needed. Even then, commodities trading had a major impact on the world by creating a global system of interrelated local markets and the cultures they represented.

Today, commodities trading has grown into a worldwide economic system in which everything from agricultural products, like wheat, oats, corn, and cattle, to industrial goods, like gold, silver, steel, and copper, are traded. It has become the major

Orange trees in Florida are iced over during a cold snap during which temperatures dropped to record-breaking lows.

mechanism by which products find their way around the world. Commodities trading helps to bring all the world's products to a global marketplace where countries can obtain the goods they need to continue to develop and thrive.

CHAPTER ONE

WHAT IS COMMODITIES TRADING?

Think about all the products we come into contact with each day. Every single one of them is produced somewhere else in the world and had to be harvested, processed, manufactured, and/or shipped to our local market or store. Oranges from Florida, oil from Saudi Arabia, coffee from Colombia, cattle from Texas, gold from Africa, and sugar from Brazil. These are just a few of the products that are traded on a daily basis. They are all in demand, and they are all commodities.

What Is a Commodity?

A commodity is a product or good that is uniform in quality and can be bought in large quantities. It is also a valuable good that is in demand. Petroleum, notebook paper, milk, cattle, oil, corn, coal, silver, copper, and steel are all examples of commodities. These goods are produced in large quantities by multiple producers and with little difference in quality between suppliers.

Oil is one of the most in-demand commodities in the world. Refineries, like the one pictured here, are located around the world. They process crude oil into products such as gasoline or diesel.

One of the characteristics of a commodity is its price. No single producer of a product can determine how much it will sell for. Instead, the price of a commodity is determined by each commodity's market. A market looks at the overall supply and

demand of a commodity. Is there a high demand for oranges? Can the supply meet that demand? If the supply cannot, the price of the commodity grows in value because there is less of it available. This was the case in 2010 when freezing weather damaged much of the orange crop. The market looks at a number of factors to determine the price of a commodity and sets a price accordingly.

Commodities are different from other products in that there is very little to differentiate them from one another. Unlike the different models of cars—which can range from a basic compact car to a luxury model that features leather seats, a stereo system, power doors and locks, and a high-end engine—there are basically no quality differences between commodities. The quality of oil mined in the state of Texas is no different than the oil mined in the country of Saudi Arabia. Copper and steel shouldn't be stronger if they are purchased from one producer over another.

There are four main categories that all commodities fall into. They are energy, metals, livestock and meat, and agriculture. The energy category includes the raw materials needed to produce energy, such as heating oil, natural gas, uranium, and gasoline. All of these are necessary to run our automobiles, heat our homes and schools, and power our companies and businesses. Metals include precious metals (gold, silver, platinum) and industrial metals (steel, copper). They are used to craft delicate jewelry, construct massive and enduring buildings and bridges, and produce precision performing cars, planes, and trucks. Livestock and meat commodities include lean hogs, pork, live cattle, and feeder cattle. The fourth category, agriculture, comprises corn, soybeans, wheat, rice, cocoa, coffee, cotton, and sugar.

Commodities are also referred to as being either soft or hard. A soft commodity is grown, like corn, wheat, rice, or coffee beans. A hard commodity is mined, like petroleum, coal, and gold.

WHAT ARE COMMODITY EXCHANGES?

Commodities trading involves the buying and selling of goods that are classified specifically as commodities. Commodities are more than just ordinary manufactured goods or products. They are also resources that are purchased for their wide range of uses. Companies around the world buy commodities to produce other products or to use the commodity itself as a resource. Corn is a popular and widely used commodity. The majority of corn produced is used as livestock feed. The remainder is processed into various food and industrial products, including starch, sweeteners such as high fructose corn syrup, corn oil, plastics, and ethanol fuel.

The New York Mercantile Exchange, located in New York City, is one of ten commodities exchanges in the United States. The commodities are traded by computer and in crowded, raucous trading pits like the one seen here.

A commodity exchange is where buyers and sellers go to trade various types of commodities. It is a marketplace that is open to the public, meaning that anyone can make trades there through a firm that is a member of the exchange. An exchange is more than just a place for commodities to be traded. It provides a number of services to both buyers and sellers. An exchange regulates the trading practices of its members, gathers and distributes price information, inspects and monitors commodities traded on the exchange, and supervises the warehouses that store commodities. It also provides a central place where disputes between buyers and sellers can be resolved. One of the exchange's most important functions is to monitor all the sales and oversee all the trading that occurs within it.

How Are Commodities Traded and What Is a Futures Contract?

Trading commodities involves the actual exchange of physical goods and/or raw materials. The commodities seller is selling actual ownership of a commodity to a buyer. However, with commodities trading, the buyer doesn't walk away from a sale with the purchase in hand, like a shopper would when he or she buys a shirt at the mall. This is because most commodities are sold in large quantities—40,000 pounds (18,144 kilograms) of lean hogs or 22,046 pounds (10,000 kg) of cocoa. Instead of buying and receiving delivery of the product directly, most commodities trading is referred to as futures trading. Futures trading lets traders buy or sell their commodity at a certain price on a particular date, with the buyer receiving shipment of the commodity at a later specified time.

The Major American Commodity Exchanges

A commodity exchange or market is a highly organized place that brings together buyers and sellers of commodities. These are six of the most important U.S. commodity exchanges trading a variety of goods.

Chicago Board of Trade: Wheat, corn, soybeans, soybean meal, silver, plywood, oats, gold, commercial paper, Treasury bonds, and Treasury notes.

Chicago Mercantile Exchange: Live cattle, fresh eggs, live hogs, lumber, potatoes, pork bellies, turkeys, and feeder cattle.

International Monetary Market: A division of the Chicago Mercantile Exchange, this market trades currency and interest rate futures.

New York Mercantile Exchange: Crude oil, natural gas, heating oil, gasoline, gold, silver, copper, aluminum, platinum, and palladium.

New York Board of Trade: Coffee, cocoa, cotton, sugar, and orange juice.

MidAmerica Commodity Exchange: This exchange is affiliated with the Chicago Board of Trade and trades grains, silver, silver coins, gold, hogs, and cattle.

13

Most commodity trading occurs with what's called a futures contract. A futures contract is an agreement between a buyer and a seller. The buyer agrees to accept delivery of a certain commodity, five thousand bushels of wheat for example, at a certain price,

Wheat is among the most popular commodities. It is sold to processors who use it to make breads, cereals, flour, and many other products used every day.

14

during a specified month of the year. A commodity and a futures contract are not one and the same. A commodity is a physical product that can be seen and touched, like corn, cattle, and cotton. A futures contract is a purchase agreement that specifies

how much the buyer will pay for a commodity in the future, say a few months from now. When someone buys a futures contract, he or she is agreeing to buy a product that will not be available until a later date.

A futures contract is similar to a cell phone plan. As a buyer, the cell phone user has signed a contract with a cell phone provider. This contract states that he or she has agreed to receive a specific set of services, such as unlimited calling minutes, text messaging, and Internet access, for a certain price each month for one year. The price will stay the same for the services agreed to for the next twelve months, regardless of whether the actual price of delivering those services increases or decreases over the year. The contract the cell phone user signs protects him or her from sudden rate increases and reduces the risk of being charged a higher

15

price. In essence, this is how a futures contract works. However, instead of services, the futures contract is for commodities.

A futures contract calls for a specific amount of a commodity to be purchased at a particular price and at a particular level

Food companies, like the Interstate Bakeries Corporation that produces Wonder Bread, buy commodities like wheat and sugar in large quantities and at set prices to ensure consistent production and pricing.

of quality. These contracts are for items a buyer is expected to need at a specific time. For example, a wheat farmer may be trying to secure a selling price for next season's crop. At the same time, a bread company may be looking ahead to next

year's production goals to determine how much wheat it needs to make its product. It will also examine how much it is able to purchase it for while still being able to make a profit once the bread is made and sold. The farmer and the bread company may enter into a futures contract requiring the delivery of a specific number of wheat bushels to the bread company during the month of June for a set per bushel price.

By entering into this futures contract, the farmer and the bread company secure a price that both parties believe will be a fair one come June. If the nationwide wheat crop is poor that year, and grain prices rise as a result, the farmer would still be obligated to accept the lower price for his or her wheat specified in the contract with the bread company. Similarly, if there is a bumper crop of wheat that year and wheat prices fall dramatically, the bread company would still be obligated to pay the higher price for the farmer's wheat agreed to in the futures contract.

It is important to note that the futures contract itself—not only the commodity—can be bought and sold in the futures market. The actual products being sold are delivered to their buyers on the dates specified in the futures contract. Yet it's the buying and selling of the futures contracts in the period before the delivery date that can make money for a commodities broker. The broker buys a futures contract and hopes the price for the commodity will rise because the contract can then be sold at a higher price than it was bought for, resulting in a profit.

CHAPTER TWO

THE WORLDWIDE EVOLUTION OF COMMODITY EXCHANGES

Buying and selling goods has been an integral part of world history since the first civilizations began to emerge thousands of years ago. Today, if we need something, we go to the nearest mall or grocery store to buy the item. Thousands of years ago, however, obtaining needed goods wasn't so simple. If the members of a community didn't grow it, herd it, or make it, they needed to find a way to obtain the item they were looking for from another community.

Back then, a farmer could trade grain for cattle or milk for goods like clothing or spices at the local market. Farmers could trade what they had for what they needed. Today, this same concept is still at work, though in a far more complicated and much more global way.

THE HISTORY OF COMMODITIES TRADING

Global commodity trading can trace its history back at least three thousand years to the Silk Road. This renowned trade route linked traders and merchants in China, India, Persia, and Mediterranean countries. They used the Silk Road to transport the silk, satin, other fine fabrics, spices, perfumes, medicine, jewels, and glassware that would be traded throughout Asia. The rise of the Roman Empire and the later medieval Crusades brought Europe into this vibrant Asian and Mediterranean trade network. And, in the sixteenth century, Europeans went in search of spices and other goods in foreign lands. At the same time, they were also seeking new, more efficient maritime trade routes to Europe, leading to the discovery of the New World.

Yet commodity trading probably goes back even further in time. For example, it is believed that Egyptians imported goats and sheep from southwest Asia in the seventh millennium BCE. Historians have also found evidence that rice futures were being traded in China six thousand years ago.

THE RISE OF THE CHICAGO EXCHANGE

Modern commodity trading began in the mid-nineteenth century, mainly in Chicago, Illinois. Chicago had an established infrastructure of railways and waterways and was located within the agricultural heartland. This made commodity shipments from midwestern farms and western ranches to eastern markets easy. All of this made the city a logical place to establish markets for the buying and selling (and delivering and shipping) of commodities.

Farmers and dealers in livestock, grain, and other agricultural products wanted a reliable way to set fair prices for their goods. Beginning in 1848, people began to grade, or rate, grain and other agricultural products to make the setting of prices easier. This enabled buyers to know and trust the quality of the product without having to examine it themselves. It was also around this time that farmers and buyers started to sign contracts in which the farmer agreed to deliver the harvest, on a specific day, at a guaranteed price to the buyer. This gave farmers the money they needed to produce their crops. Buyers received the product at a set price and on a set schedule.

It was out of this early form of agricultural business transactions that commodity trading grew and exchanges, or the markets where goods could be bought and sold, were founded. The Chicago Board of Trade (CBOT) was established in 1848 to help manage the unpredictable grain market in the midwestern United States.

At the time, prices for agricultural products were ruled by boom and bust cycles. During the winter months, when grain was scarce and the weather limited farmers' ability to grow more crops, prices rose. During the summer and fall months, when crops were harvested, farmers came to Chicago to sell their crops. So many farmers were looking to sell their goods that they overwhelmed the city and the trading posts. The markets were flooded with agricultural produce, so prices collapsed as supply far exceeded demand. Some farmers were unable to find buyers and went home empty handed. Others received very low prices since the supply was so great. The cost of planting, raising, harvesting, and transporting the crop to market may have been higher than the price they received for the crop. This would mean they lost money on the crop.

As a result, the CBOT was created to help farmers get a guaranteed price for their goods. Farmers could now negotiate a set price for the crop they would harvest later, regardless of

The Chicago Mercantile Exchange was founded in 1898. Today, it is the largest futures exchange in the United States and the second largest in the world.

what the supply and demand situation was once the delivery time came. Meanwhile, buyers were ensured a specific quantity of a crop they needed at harvest time. If the crop did poorly that year and supplies were low, they were at least guaranteed

delivery of the quantity of wheat they had agreed to buy from the farmer. They wouldn't have to scramble with thousands of other buyers to find a supply of the crop at extremely high prices.

GLOBAL COMMODITIES MARKETS

Today, there are ten commodity exchanges in the United States. The largest are the Chicago Board of Trade, the Chicago Mercantile Exchange, the New York Mercantile Exchange, the New York Commodity Exchange, and the New York Coffee, Sugar, and Cocoa Exchange. Worldwide, there are major exchanges in more than twenty countries, including Canada, England, France, Singapore, Japan, India, Australia, and New Zealand. These international exchanges trade everything from agricultural products to rubber, beans, and gold.

While these exchanges trade a number of well-established products, like wheat, steel, cattle, oil, and corn, exchanges are always looking for new products to trade. Carbon, a chemical

23

On the trading floor, commodity traders barter for goods using a series of hand gestures to communicate with other traders. The floor can be a fast and furious, yet exciting, environment in which to work.

element, has become one of the world's fastest-growing new commodities. But not all new commodities introduced are successful in the markets. Tiger shrimp and cheddar cheese are two products that both failed to establish themselves as commodity goods and are no longer traded as such.

WHAT COMMODITIES ARE TRADED?

Commodities trading in Chicago originally focused on agricultural products. Today, in addition to these, the CBOT also trades metals, lumber, and dairy products. Markets located around the world trade a wide variety of these and other commodities.

Worldwide Commodities Exchanges

Commodities exchanges are located around the world partly because countries are always looking for new buyers and new ways to get their products into the global marketplace. Globalization and the increase in the trade of products worldwide have increased the number of international commodities exchanges.

Commodities markets help countries organize the production, sale, shipment, and delivery of their goods. They also establish a reliable and trusted place to sell goods and negotiate fair prices. Here is a sample of some of the commodities exchanges around the world and the products each exchange specializes in.

Country	Exchange	Commodities
Brazil	Brazilian Mercantile and Futures Exchange	Agricultural goods, precious metals
England	London Metal Exchange	Industrial metals, plastics
Ethiopia	Ethiopia Commodity Exchange	Coffee, corn, wheat
Hong Kong	Hong Kong Mercantile Exchange	Gold
Iran	Iranian Oil Bourse	Oil, gas, petrochemicals
Nigeria	Abuja Securities and Commodity Exchange	Corn, grain
Singapore	Singapore Commodity Exchange	Agricultural products, rubber
United Arab Emirates (Dubai)	Dubai Mercantile Exchange	Energy
USA (Chicago)	Chicago Board of Trade	Grain, livestock, and dairy

Agricultural commodities: Agricultural commodities include goods such as corn, soybeans, ethanol, oats, cocoa, wheat, cotton, and rice. These products are traded in standard amounts and at a set quality. Agricultural commodities are traded in their

Cattle and other livestock, like sheep and pigs, are important and heavily traded commodities. They are purchased by food processors and fabric and cloth manufacturers.

raw and/or unprocessed state. So a buyer can purchase wheat, but not flour, which is a product made from wheat.

Precious metals: The most common precious metals are gold and silver, but this category also includes platinum and palladium. These commodities are always sold by the ounce.

Industrial metals: This category includes copper, lead, zinc, tin, aluminum, nickel, and steel. These metals are sold by the metric ton, which is 1,000 kilograms or 2,204.6 pounds. The London Metal Exchange is the world's premier industrial metals market.

Livestock and meat: Lean hogs, frozen pork bellies, and live cattle are all commodities traded in 20 ton (20,000 kg), or 40,000 pound, units.

Energy commodities: Crude oil, natural gas, heating oil, propane, and ethanol are all energy commodities that are traded.

New commodities are added periodically to a market. As long as there is uncertainty—and anxiety—concerning the future price and supply of a given commodity, there will be an interest in trading futures contracts for that commodity.

THE IMPORTANCE OF MARKET REGULATION

For commodity trading to work efficiently, there needs to be confidence in how the system as a whole works. Commodity trading is regulated. This helps ensure that no matter what product is sought, a broker can work toward securing it for a fair price knowing that all of the products in that category are of the same quality. Regulating commodities evens the playing field for everyone. It ensures fair prices and helps protect the buyer from purchasing an inferior product.

For example, if a commodities broker is acting on behalf of a manufacturing company that requires copper to make electrical wiring, the broker is going to seek out the best price for the amount of copper that his or her client needs. If all of the traders are offering copper of the same quality, a broker can simply watch the price of copper as it rises and falls based on supply and demand. The broker can then make the decision if and when to buy based only on price, without concern for whether the copper is of poor, fair, good, or excellent quality.

In the United States, commodity trading is overseen and regulated by the Commodity Futures Trading Commission, a

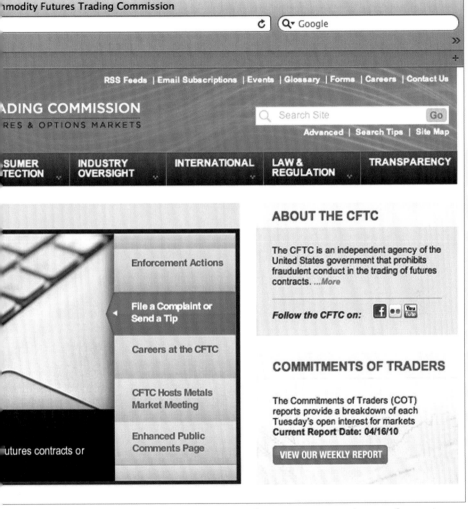

The U.S. Commodity Futures Trading Commission (www.cftc.gov) oversees commodity trading in the United States. The group regulates the trading industry and ensures that high standards are met.

federal agency. Created by Congress in 1974, the commission is in place to protect buyers and sellers against exploitation, unfair trade practices, and fraud. It also helps to maintain the integrity (fairness) of commodities pricing. The Commodity Futures Trading Commission is an agency of the U.S. Department of Agriculture.

In addition to overseeing commodities markets, the agency also regulates the futures exchanges, brokerage firms, money managers, and commodity advisers who employ brokers or monitor trades. Perhaps the biggest role the commission has is to establish standards for commodities. The quality of all commodities traded at an exchange must be equal between all sellers. This helps to guarantee product quality while protecting the buyer from fraudulent purchases. Traders don't want to buy one hundred units of cattle only to find out that the animals are infected with disease or that the sugar purchased is of inferior or unacceptable quality.

CHAPTER THREE

THE INSIDER'S GUIDE TO COMMODITIES TRADING

Trading commodities and futures contracts is not only a mechanism by which products find their way to the people, companies, or communities that need them throughout the world. It is a profession that can be exciting and frenetic (fast-paced) and requires split-second decision-making abilities. Commodities trading is also a way to make money.

While a person can make a lot of money trading commodities, it's an activity that requires skill, knowledge, and savvy decision-making. It can be a risky game to play. A lot of money can be lost if a trader doesn't understand how trading works, how commodity prices rise and fall, and when the best times to buy and sell are.

BEING IN THE KNOW

To begin trading commodities, one needs to open an account with a commodities broker. A commodities broker is an individual who is authorized to buy or sell commodities on behalf

Commodity brokers gather on the floor of the Kansas City Board of Trade, where they will buy and sell commodities for their clients.

of a client. Brokers often advise their clients on what commodities to buy and sell and when to do so.

To make good decisions on when to buy or sell a given commodity, brokers often refer to price and trend information.

This data can be found in financial newspapers such as the *Wall Street Journal* and *Investors Business Daily*. Financial Web sites such as Bloomberg.com, Turtletrader.com, and Purchasing.com also provide commodities data, as do online industry magazines such as Commodity News (commodityonline.com) and Stocks & Commodities magazine (traders.com). There are also industry-wide, commodity-specific resources that track price fluctuations such as agricultural products (agweb.com), cotton (cotloook.com), steel (steelonthenet.com), and gold (gold-miningstocks.com).

Once brokers decide that it's the best time to make a transaction for a given commodity, they contact one of the exchanges where that particular commodity is bought and sold. Not every exchange trades every commodity. Many specialize in certain goods. The New York Mercantile Exchange trades only energy, precious metals, and industrial metals. The Kansas Board of Trade deals only with agricultural commodities, while the Hong Kong Mercantile Exchange's sole focus is gold.

Determining How and When to Make a Trade

Before considering a trade, one must become knowledgeable about the commodity and the market. Is a particular commodity selling for a high price right now? Why might that be happening? How long are prices likely to continue to rise? What commodities are about to go lower in price? Why are they about to go lower? How low will they go before they rise again? These are just a few questions commodities traders might ask themselves as they look at what to trade and when.

There are two primary methods for deciding when to trade a given commodity. These are fundamental analysis and technical analysis. Fundamental analysis uses economic information relating to supply and demand to predict the future price of a commodity. For example, freezing temperatures in Florida in January mean a smaller crop of oranges at harvest time. With a smaller supply available, the price of oranges will increase because the demand will be greater than the available supply. If a trader has access to reliable long-term weather predictions based on sophisticated and accurate computer modeling, he or she might buy an orange futures contract in October in which the price for the oranges was based on

To make educated decisions, commodity traders rely on sophisticated software that helps traders predict pricing patterns and demand.

current, relatively low orange prices. Then if the freeze the trader expects arrives in January and the orange crop is damaged, the value of the contract will rise greatly as the price of oranges come harvesttime will skyrocket due to decreased supply.

Technical analysis, on the other hand, involves analyzing past prices of commodities to predict a future price. Memorial Day, the unofficial start of the summer car travel season, always sees increases in the price of gasoline. Because demand for gas rises in the summer months, prices rise to take advantage of high demand. People are willing to pay higher prices because they have no choice—they are traveling on vacation and will buy gas no matter what the price. This is a predictable annual upward swing in prices that just as predictably begins to fall come Labor Day and the unofficial end of summer travel season. Using this trend data, a commodities trader can successfully predict that oil prices will increase this year in the weeks before Memorial Day. The time to buy an oil futures contract would be several weeks before Memorial Day and the time to sell it would be as prices hit their summer peak.

Most successful commodities traders emphasize technical analysis in their decision-making. This is because obtaining fundamental data can be difficult. Often, it can also be inaccurate. While there are various resources that publish statistics on the supply and availability of certain commodities and the demand for them, this information is largely based on estimates and educated guesses. It is not usually based on actual, hard data concerning the size of a certain crop for the upcoming season or the amount of gold that will be mined in the next year.

Clients begin the trading process by contacting their broker and telling him or her how much of a particular commodity they want to buy or sell. The broker then places the order on a computer.

Or, if the broker works on the exchange's trading floor, he or she will trade directly with other floor traders. The broker executes the sale with other traders on the exchange floor by using a combination of shouting and hand signals. Once a trade is made, the broker communicates the sale information directly to his or her client.

How to Make Money on Commodities

The Internet has made the world of commodity trading available to anyone with a computer. This has helped commodities trading grow exponentially over the last decade. These are the general guidelines on how to succeed and make money trading commodities:

- **Buy low and sell high:** Traders will make money if they buy a commodity at a low price and sell it when the price increases.
- **What goes up must come down:** When prices rise quickly and to high levels, they almost always drop just as quickly. Taking advantage of these extremes helps people make money on trades. But it also requires them to watch the market carefully and make quick decisions, selling off their contract before the commodity price falls again.
- **Don't overthink the market:** The rise and fall of prices is not always rational and might not always have a clear explanation behind it. Sometimes all that traders need to know is what direction prices are moving in (up or down) and how long it has been happening. A prolonged decrease or increase in prices is likely to run its course and be reversed.

TRADING STRATEGIES

Commodity trading can be very profitable for those with the skills, knowledge, and experience to make smart and savvy trades. There are three common strategies to trading that most traders follow. They are basic technical analysis, pure speculation, and supply and demand.

Basic technical analysis: Many traders rely on this strategy because it incorporates a lot of key information, such as trading volume, historical analysis of high and low prices, and estimations of whether the commodity's price will rise or fall. This strategy does not incorporate important factors like market demand or innovation. Instead, it strictly uses chart data and trends.

Pure speculation: Some commodity traders employ a strategy called pure speculation. It is based on what people think might happen. For example, a speculator might think that the Atlantic storm season will be particularly damaging to off-shore oil production, or that

states in the Midwest might experience increased tornado and hail activity, destroying various crops. By betting on bad weather (whether based on actual long-range meteorological forecasts or mere hunches), a speculator could buy commodity

Unforeseen disasters, such as bad weather, can damage agricultural commodities. They can also increase the price for a commodity if the damage is widespread and lessens the supply available to traders.

futures on the expectation that the prices will rise because of damage to a commodity's supply.

Supply and demand: There are some events that are seasonal activities that are always expected to occur. For example, Americans drive more in the summer than they do at other times of the year. This seasonal increase in demand for gasoline results in seasonal increases in price. A trader who pursues a supply and demand strategy might use this information to buy oil in the spring. The trader would then sell it in the summer when he or she is pretty certain prices will rise because demand will almost certainly increase.

How a Futures Contract Works

Trading commodities is also known as futures trading. This is because commodities traders are essentially betting on the future price of a given commodity once it is harvested or produced. This "wager" is also a bet on what the supply of that commodity will be on a specified future date and what the demand will be, and therefore how the price will rise or fall to reflect that supply and demand.

Here is an example to illustrate how the trading process works. The ABC Gold Company wants to sell 100 ounces (2.8 kg) of gold it will mine by August. XYZ Jewelry Makers needs to buy 100 ounces of gold to make gold rings and bracelets that it wants to start manufacturing in September. Both companies are looking ahead on the calendar and making their buying and selling plans accordingly. It's only February, which means there is still a lot of time before ABC needs to sell its gold and XYZ needs to buy it.

How to Become a Commodities Broker

A commodities broker is a financial services professional who is licensed to sell commodities. Unlike a stockbroker, who deals only with stock—shares of ownership in a company—a commodity broker deals with physical goods. These can include foods, metals, energy sources, building materials, and agricultural products.

To become a broker, a person needs to pass a series of exams. These exams test knowledge of the market, hedging, futures contracts, orders, options, and most aspects of trading. They also test one's knowledge of the laws and policies that regulate commodities trading. Every commodity broker is licensed and registered with the National Futures Association, an organization that develops rules, programs, and services to help brokers do their jobs in a legal, reputable, and ethical manner.

Most commodity brokers work for brokerage firms that specialize in commodities. For example, stock brokerage firms do not trade commodities. Chicago is the unofficial headquarters for U.S. commodities trading. It is home to the two largest exchanges in the United States, the Chicago Board of Trade and the Chicago Mercantile Exchange. Because of this, Chicago has a number of firms that hire commodities brokers. These include Pearl and Redford Trading of Chicago, A/C Trading Company, and Central States Commodities, Inc. Most major North American cities have a small number of commodity brokerage firms as well, as do most nations. This enables commodities brokers to work nearly anywhere in the country or around the world.

The price of gold could rise or fall significantly between February and August. If ABC Gold Company waits until August to sell its 100 ounces of gold, it might run the risk of the price of gold dropping, resulting in less profit from the sale. However, if XYZ Jewelry Makers waits to buy its needed gold, it runs the risk of paying a higher price if gold prices rise. This would cause XYZ to make less money selling the jewelry made from this gold. This is why both parties agree on a futures contract. The contract limits the risk for both the buyer and the seller. It establishes a fair price for both companies. Most important, it ensures a sale for ABC Jewelry Company and guarantees a supply of precious metal for XYZ Jewelry Makers by the time it needs the gold.

CHAPTER FOUR

THE ECONOMIC PRINCIPLES BEHIND COMMODITIES TRADING

The commodities markets, both historically and in modern times, have had a major impact on the world's nations and on world history. Commodity shortages have even caused wars throughout history. For example, in the 1930s, Japan invaded Manchuria (Northern China) in search of raw materials, including coal, oil, and iron.

Shortages and scarcity of basic commodities can cause great human suffering and conflict. Yet the overabundance of a commodity can also have a devastating effect. If prices drop so low that the overabundant commodity becomes virtually worthless, this can lead to personal financial ruin and larger economic collapse. For example, the effects of the Great Depression were worsened for farmers when certain crops that they had been overproducing glutted the market. Because they couldn't turn a profit on these devalued crops, farm foreclosures increased and farmers were forced off their land. This swelled the westward tide of homeless migrant agricultural workers that had begun when overfarming of the soil had created Dust Bowl conditions. Once fertile farmland that had fed the world became barren wastelands of depleted dirt. This worsened the effects of the global depression by decreasing the quantity and quality of the world's food supply.

Commodities have always played a major role in our global economy. They affect the lives of every one of us, no matter where we live. Understanding the basic principles of economics helps us understand how and why commodities have the powerful impact that they do.

THE LAW OF SUPPLY AND DEMAND

One of the most basic economic principles is the law of supply and demand. It governs every business, everywhere, no matter what type of product it manufactures or grows.

Demand refers to the amount of a product that is needed or wanted by buyers. It also reflects how much people are willing and able to pay for a desired product. Supply refers to the amount of product available for purchase. Together, supply

44

and demand determine price. Commodity trading is based on supply, demand, and the expected future prices of products. The lower supply there is of a given commodity, the higher the demand and the more money people are willing to pay for

ORGANIC
GROWN IN MICHIGAN

Organic
Braeburn
Apples

$2.69

WHOLE FOODS   PLU 94103   PER POUND

Organic produce is growing in demand, despite a limited supply. This means grocery stores can charge a premium (high) price for the product.

the item. Even if demand doesn't increase but remains the same, a smaller supply will mean an increase in prices.

There are many things that can impact supply and demand. A farmer has only so much land to grow crops on. If the population is growing and more people need food, then the demand for the farmer's product will increase, as will the price he receives for it. Major disruptions in supply (known as supply shocks), such as widespread livestock diseases or weather-damaged crops, can affect the supply of products. Supply shocks reduce the amount of a product that is available, which also increases the product's price. All of these outside influences impact the supply of a product, its demand, and the price at which the commodity can sell for.

PLANNING AHEAD

The buying of commodities is essential to any company that relies on a given commodity as an ingredient in or component of the product that it manufactures or produces. By agreeing in advance to buy a certain quantity of that commodity at a certain price, a manufacturer can plan for production (and the costs of production). The manufacturer can do so without having to worry about the fluctuation in prices or available supply of the materials or goods required to make the product it sells.

For example, a leading cereal manufacturer needs to buy wheat, corn, and oats to produce its different types of cereal products. By purchasing these commodities through futures trading, the company can secure fair prices for the ingredients it needs as it plans the amount of cereal it will produce over the next six to twelve months. Commodities trading makes it possible for the cereal company to plan its production without having to worry about whether or not it will receive a shipment of ingredients or if the price of the ingredients will increase unexpectedly.

However, future trading can drive the prices of commodities up. As mentioned earlier, severe weather in Florida negatively affects the state's orange groves. Speculators are financial experts who guess, or speculate, on the future price of a commodity. Speculators could raise prices on the sale of oranges because they know demand will remain steady for a supply that might be smaller due to the bad weather. Anyone who bought a futures contract for oranges before the freezing weather and the resulting price increase will have secured a guaranteed supply of the fruit at a bargain price.

ESTABLISHING COMMODITY PRICES

Prices for commodities can and do fluctuate. The market itself can impact the price of a commodity, as can traders who may influence a price by creating unreasonable expectations.

A market establishes the prices of goods. This helps to even out the playing field between large corporations selling commodities and smaller, family-owned businesses. When the market sets the price, it stays the same no matter who is selling the commodity. The only negative aspect of this is that financial growth can be limited because sellers are not able to set their own prices for the goods they are selling. Traders can also influence the price of a commodity. This can affect the price consumers pay by the time the product gets to the grocery store, gas pump, or shopping mall.

In economics there's the law of one price. This law essentially says that if a market is efficient then a good should have only

Traders rely on a variety of information—from Web sites and software to professional experience—to make educated buying and selling decisions.

one price. For example, whatever price commodities traders are trading oil for, that should also be the price that suppliers (sellers) and oil refineries (buyers) see. If the law of one price was not in effect, then there would be huge differences

in the price of oil from seller to seller. The buying and selling of oil would be a chaotic process, with sellers trying to undercut each other and buyers spending most of their time bargain hunting and haggling.

Without this law in effect, a trader could buy oil for one price in one market and sell it for a higher price in another. This would result in cutthroat wheeling and dealing, and the end result would be wildly confusing consumer prices. By the time products reached the stores, there would be no rhyme or reason to the pricing because different manufacturers paid different prices for the same commodities and raw materials that were used to make the products. Those manufacturers who paid a higher price for the commodity would have to charge more for their finished product in order to make a profit. Those manufacturers who had paid less for the commodity could charge less for their product but still make a good profit, while attracting bargain-hunting consumers away from the higher-priced competition.

Bioethanol is an alternative fuel source that can be used in place of gasoline to fuel cars. If it grows in popularity, it could lessen the demand for crude oil, thereby increasing the supply of oil and lowering its price.

Product Innovation and Increased Demand

The creation of new products and energy fuels can increase the demand for existing commodities that could now be used in new ways. For example, prices for oil had been rising steadily throughout the early years of the 2000s. For the last several decades, the United States has had ongoing conflicts in the Middle East, a prime location for oil supplies and refineries. As oil prices grew out of control, alternative energy sources began to look promising as a way to lessen North American dependence upon Middle Eastern oil to fuel cars, heat homes, and power factories and businesses. One of the most popular alternative fuel sources to emerge was ethanol, which is produced from corn. As ethanol production and use grew, prices for corn began to rise sharply.

Should demand for corn continue to grow in the years ahead due to ethanol production, corn prices will be driven higher. Likely, this will result in farmers planting more corn at the expense of other crops, such as soybeans and wheat, to accommodate the increasing demand. This will create scarcity of soybeans and wheat and an increase in their prices.

Because so much of the corn will be dedicated to fuel use, the supply of corn for food will shrink. This will be so even though demand among livestock and poultry producers, cereal companies, and other manufacturers that rely on corn as an ingredient for their products will continue to grow. Consumers will also feel the effect of higher corn prices at the grocery store. This is because the higher cost of the commodity will be passed down to everyone who buys cereal, bread, chicken, and any of the many thousands of food and industrial products made with the help of corn.

MYTHS and FACTS

MYTH I'm going to get a load of corn delivered to my house if I trade in corn futures.

FACT When trading commodities, brokers often buy and sell the futures contract, not the commodity itself. So you may buy a futures contract for forty thousand bushels of corn, but that doesn't mean you bought that much corn or that it will be delivered to you. Before the delivery date of the corn, you would probably sell the contract, hopefully for more than you paid for it. You will sell it to someone who actually wanted the corn (like a cornmeal manufacturer) or to another trader who also hoped to make money off the contract before the corn's delivery date.

MYTH You need a lot of money to become a commodities trader.

FACT Many commodity brokers will allow you to open a trading account with as little as $5,000. Some accounts may be started with even less cash on hand.

MYTH You can lose a lot of money trading commodities.

FACT While commodities trading is a risky investment and you can lose some or all of the money that you put into it, many brokers make money and see big profits. It is normally the professional commodity traders and experienced money managers who consistently make money year after year by doing their research and following a strict and disciplined trading plan.

CHAPTER FIVE

WHAT AFFECTS COMMODITY SUPPLY AND PRICES?

Commodities trading is the primary mechanism by which raw goods are distributed around the country and the world. There are many factors than can affect commodity supplies and their prices, in both positive and negative ways.

CRUDE OIL

Crude oil is one of the most in-demand commodities worldwide. The supply of oil is carefully controlled by oil-producing nations. They make sure that the available supply never greatly exceeds the demand, so prices won't slump. Reduction in oil outputs from wells around the world can lead to upward surges in oil prices. Decreased demand—due to either the viability of alternative energy sources or reduced driving and industrial manufacturing during an economic recession, for example—can drive prices down.

The slightest variation in the price of crude oil can have a major influence on the economy of many countries. During price slumps, oil-producing nations lose significant income, while oil-consuming nations enjoy extra savings. Similarly, during price spikes, the finances of oil-consuming nations can be stretched thin, while oil-producing nations are awash in cash.

Emerging Nations

Global economic development is also having an effect on the commodities market. The emergence of China and India as significant economic players has contributed to an increase in demand—and in prices—for commodities such as steel, copper, and other industrial metals. Rapidly developing and

Fuel prices can fluctuate greatly based on supply and demand. In China, drivers crowded into a gas station when news broke that gas prices were about to rise sharply.

industrializing nations require these materials to build new homes, schools, office buildings, manufacturing plants, and other commercial properties. As these nations' populations continue to grow, the prices of other commodities, such as aluminum, sugar, and corn, will also rise with increased demand. In these cases, demand can far outstrip supply, even when the supply is not necessarily small.

India and China are both experiencing huge technological and cultural changes. China's population represents the largest number of mobile-phone users in the entire world. They also log the second-highest amount of time on the Internet. India is not far behind. As a result, demand for energy—mostly coal and oil—is increasing in these countries and is expected to continue to rise throughout at least the first half of the twenty-first century.

Technological Advances

New advances in technology and innovation impact the price and supply of commodities, as well as the demand for them. Ethanol, an alternative fuel created from corn, reduces U.S. dependence on imported oil, is better for the environment, and has decreased gasoline prices. New energy resources, such as wind, solar, and biofuel, are being developed to lessen North America's dependence on foreign oil. As these energy sources grow in popularity and are made available to the public for use, North American demand for crude oil will decrease, driving down oil prices worldwide.

The same can be said of hybrid and electric cars, which run on either a combination of gasoline and electricity or electricity alone. These automobiles rely significantly less on gasoline as

As alternative energy sources become more popular, the demand for carbon-based energy decreases. Here, solar energy panels on an apartment building offset the need for oil and gas for heating and electricity.

their main energy source. As hybrid and electric cars, trucks, and buses grow in popularity, the demand for oil as a transportation fuel will diminish, and oil prices should fall as a result.

Computer Trading Glitches

Commodity trading has become more dependent on computers than ever before. Today, there is a wide rage of software that has been developed to help commodities brokers research goods, track prices, provide historical analysis, and guide informed decision-making. Sales are conducted almost exclusively by computer now.

Because the market is computer-driven, breakdowns in technology, security issues, and software malfunction can affect trading and create major problems. When computers crash, trading is halted. And when trading halts, no one is buying or selling, and no one is making any money. Millions of dollars in sales can be lost in mere minutes. Global commodities markets and prices can be affected by a shutdown of any one commodity market.

Interesting Facts About Commodities Trading

- One hundred years ago, there were more than one thousand commodity exchanges in the United States. Today, there are only ten.
- The New York Mercantile Exchange trades billions of dollars worth of metals and other precious commodities every day.
- The Sydney Futures Exchange, located in Sydney, Australia, is the tenth largest commodities exchange in the world.
- Corn, cotton, oats, rice, and soybeans are the most traded agricultural commodities in the world.
- The Chicago Mercantile Exchange is known throughout the world as the largest futures and options exchange.
- There are new commodities added to exchanges on a regular basis, though not all of them succeed.

UNFORESEEN DISASTERS

Unusual weather patterns, natural disasters, epidemics, and human-made disasters can impact commodity trading or bring it to a halt altogether. There have been several instances over the years when unforeseen events have impacted the production of commodities, as well as the global trading of them.

In 2005, an epidemic of mad cow disease struck many herds in the United Kingdom. A large portion of cattle in the

After an *E. coli* outbreak in spinach, a wholesale fruit and vegetable dealer handles produce that will need to be destroyed.

United Kingdom had to be destroyed to prevent the spread of the disease to other cattle and to prevent people from eating infected meat. The United Kingdom's supply of cattle dropped significantly. This forced countries like Russia and South Africa, which ordinarily bought cattle on the commodities market from the United Kingdom, to look elsewhere for beef. They turned to Australia, which was a large supplier of beef to the United States. A lower supply of cattle from the United Kingdom led to an increase in the demand for Australian cattle. This resulted in less beef for the United States and an increase in prices for cattle since demand was high and global supplies lower than usual. In turn, this meant that prices of beef and beef products in supermarkets rose as well.

Fresh vegetables are generally considered safe food products to eat. However, in 2006, an *E. coli* outbreak occurred in bagged spinach grown in California, where almost 75 percent of the nation's fresh spinach and 67 percent of canned and frozen spinach are grown. The U.S. Food and Drug Administration called for bagged spinach and any other products that contained fresh spinach to be pulled from grocery store shelves around the country after several people became ill from ingesting the contaminated produce. The outbreak led to increased prices for produce as a whole, as restaurants, grocery stores, and other businesses that use spinach replaced the ingredient with other leafy greens and vegetables. With spinach supply dropping extremely low virtually overnight, the price for it skyrocketed as demand increased.

CHAPTER SIX

GLOBALIZATION'S EFFECT ON COMMODITIES TRADING

Globalization has tied commodity markets together worldwide. This is both a positive and a negative development. On the plus side, it has leveled out the playing field in terms of the prices of goods. No one country can seek a higher price for a given product since there are now multiple commodities exchanges and traders to go to in order to obtain that product. If one country charges an unreasonably high price, traders can simply go elsewhere to trade for that product. However, because of globalized markets and trading, when there is a drop in a commodity's supply in one locality, it can raise the price of the good for everyone worldwide.

Oil and the War in Iraq

Oil is one of the world's most important and popular commodities. It is the major source of energy for the world's population and its homes, offices, and industries. It is needed to fuel our cars and heat our homes, it provides the energy for

With 50 percent of oil supplies used to fuel cars and trucks, the growth of developing nations—and the increased number of vehicles on the road worldwide—will increase demand for oil, raising its price.

manufacturing companies to produce goods, and it is necessary for industrial development.

More than 50 percent of oil demand is for transportation purposes. With car ownership on the rise in developing countries like China and India, the demand is only expected to increase. It is estimated that by 2050, there will be more than 1.1 billion cars on the road around the world. To put that huge number in perspective, in 2005 there were only twenty million cars being driven around the world. That enormous increase in automobile usage will raise the demand for oil. While alternative fuel sources, such as fuel cells and ethanol, are being developed, they may never fully replace or even directly impact our global demand for oil. When there is a limited supply of a commodity coupled with a rapidly increasing demand, the result is ever-increasing prices.

Oil is a global commodity, and because the world depends on it, an interruption of its supply affects everyone, everywhere. It is estimated that on average the world uses more than seventy-six million barrels of oil a day. The war in Iraq that began in 2003 had a large impact on the global supply of oil. Outside of Saudi Arabia, Iraq and Iran possess the two biggest oil reserves in the world. The Iraq War caused the price of oil to surge to record high prices. In 2003, when the United States first invaded Iraq, the price of a barrel of oil was around $25. By 2010, that price had risen to nearly $100 per barrel. For consumers, this means filling their cars with gas costs more, as does heating their homes in the winter.

GOLD AND THE RECESSION OF 2008–2010

During the global recession of 2008–2010, the value of the U.S. dollar dropped. But the same wasn't true for the value of gold. In fact, the price of gold increased as the dollar slipped. Investors were seeking to put their money into gold. This is because gold is seen as a commodity that retains (or even increases) its value in bad economic times, when other world currencies are losing their value and spending power.

The biggest factors influencing the price of gold are its supply (the astounding amount of the precious metal held in banks around the world) and its demand. Banks hold gold because its value is determined by supply and demand, unlike other investments such as currencies, whose values are set by governments and influenced by fiscal policy. For commodities

During periods of recession, the value of gold typically rises as currency values fall. As a result, many people sell their gold jewelry during hard economic times to take advantage of the increased profit they can make.

traders, buying gold when it is priced lower—just before the value of currencies slip—and selling when its price increases is the goal. Buying gold is a great way to ride out a recession until currencies rebound and regain some value.

During the recession of 2008–2010, opportunities emerged for the average person to make money on gold trading without actually having to become a commodities trader. Television commercials and newspaper ads began popping up, advertising businesses offering to buy unwanted and broken gold jewelry. The companies running these ads, along with jewelry stores, pawnshops, and online gold buyers, take the gold that ordinary people sell to them and resell it to refineries. The refineries melt the gold down into bullion (bars or ingots) that can then be sold privately or in the commodities market.

BANNED CHICKEN

In the latter half of the first decade of the 2000s, a marked reduction in the demand for chicken was observed. This decrease in demand had nothing to do with the global recession. Instead it concerned international trade relations.

Russia, one of the largest importers of U.S. chicken, placed a ban on the product. It barred the meat from entering the country after reducing its limit on the amount of chlorine U.S. processors were allowed to use to disinfect the meat. This pushed more chicken back into the U.S. market, where it competed with beef for consumers' dollars. Because the market was suddenly flooded with chickens, the cost decreased, making chicken an even more tempting alternative to higher priced beef. What was a setback for U.S. chicken producers was a boon to American families.

FALLING COFFEE PRICES

Coffee has grown in popularity as a beverage. There are more than 100 million people who drink coffee and coffee-based drinks, like mochaccino and frappuccino, every day. Coffee is the world's second most popular drink, after water.

When a leading chain of coffee shops in the United States began growing in popularity, it suddenly had more cash at its disposal. The company decided that instead of buying coffee from plantation owners in various equatorial countries around

During the 1980s and 1990s, coffee enjoyed a long stretch as a high-value commodity, thanks to the growing popularity of coffee bars. Recent changes in coffee production, however, have lowered average selling prices.

the globe via commodity trading, it would instead buy its own coffee plantations. Because of this, the overall global supply for coffee rose, since the farmers who once supplied this coffee chain with beans were now free to sell to other companies. The sudden but enduring increase in the supply of coffee beans lowered prices for the commodity over the long term.

THE RISE OF INDUSTRIAL METALS

Countries around the world are growing in terms of both population and industrialization. India and China are just two countries that have become manufacturing powerhouses. Many other developing nations are also making rapid industrial and technological leaps forward. As more and more countries become industrialized, more industrial metals—such as steel, aluminum, tin, and copper—are required. They are needed for the construction of their buildings, bridges, homes, roads, power grids, telecommunications, and other vital infrastructure.

Speculation is helping to drive up the prices of industrial metals. Speculators are estimating that demand from China, currently the world's biggest consumer of aluminum and copper, will continue to grow. Because of its multiple uses, copper has become the world's most heavily traded industrial metal. Copper is used to produce alloys such as brass and bronze, which are a combination of several types of metals. Copper is also used widely for electrical purposes and in electronics. More than 74 percent of the copper that is produced is used in building construction.

COMMODITIES MAKE THE WORLD GO ROUND

Learning how commodities trading works helps us to understand how the world functions as a whole. No country will ever be able to make, plant, or manufacture everything it needs to survive. In addition, many of the commodities we need on a global scale are found only in certain parts of the world. As long as our society continues to grow and expand, so will our dependence on trading commodities to furnish our needs and wants. Once we understand what commodities are, how they are traded and why, it is easy to see how closely tied all of the world's nations are to one another.

Ten Great Questions
to Ask a Financial Adviser

1. Why are commodities a smart investment?

2. What is your experience with commodities trading?

3. How do I make money from trading commodities?

4. Are you the best person to guide me in making decisions about buying and selling commodities?

5. Can I trade commodities at any exchange around the world or just those located in the Unites States?

6. How much money do I need if I want to start trading commodities?

7. How much money can I make from trading commodities? How much can I lose?

8. How is the money I make from commodities trading taxed?

9. How much risk is involved in trading commodities?

10. Can you put me in touch with a trusted and proven commodities broker?

GLOSSARY

alloy A metal that is made from more than one substance.

broker An individual who is paid a fee or commission for executing buy or sell orders for a customer. A commodities broker can manage client accounts, make trade recommendations, and place trades.

buyer Someone who is interested in purchasing a commodity.

commodities exchange A place where various goods and products are traded.

commodity A product that is uniform in quality and can be bought in large quantities; a good for which there is demand.

delivery The transfer of a commodity from the seller to the buyer of a futures contract.

demand A desire for a particular good or product.

developing country A nation with a low level of material well-being, but that has the potential to grow.

export Good and services that are provided by one country and shipped for sale to another.

futures contract An agreement to buy or sell a specific commodity, detailing the amount and grade of the product, the price of the product, and the date when the product will be delivered to the buyer.

import Goods and services that are brought into a country.

industrial metals Metals such as titanium, steel, copper, lead, and zinc; these are traded as commodities.

recession A decline in activity across the economy, lasting longer than a few months.

seller A person who offers a commodity for sale.

speculator A person who guesses whether a commodity will increase or decrease in price over a certain period of time.

supply The total amount of a specific good that is available to consumers.

trading volume The overall number of futures contracts traded over a specified period of time during a trading day.

FOR MORE INFORMATION

American Commodity Distribution Association (ACDA)
11358 Barley Field Way
Marriottsville, MD 21104
(410) 442-4612
Web site: http://www.commodityfoods.org
A nonprofit professional trade association, the ACDA is
   devoted to improving the U.S. Department of Agriculture's
   Commodity Food Distribution Program.

Canadian Council of Grocery Distributors
6455 Jean-Talon East, Suite 402
Montreal, QC H1S 3E8
Canada
Web site: http://www.ccgd.ca
The Canadian Council of Grocery Distributors is a not-for-
   profit organization committed to advancing and promoting
   the grocery and food service distribution industry in
   Canada, at both regional and national levels.

CME Group
20 South Wacker Drive
Chicago, IL 60606
(312) 930-1000
Web site: http://www.cmegroup.com

CME Group is the world's largest and most diverse marketplace for derivatives, including futures. The group controls
the Chicago Board of Trade, which first created futures
contracts.

Food & Consumer Products of Canada (FCPC)
885 Don Mills Road, Suite 301
Toronto, ON M3C 1V9
Canada
(416) 510-8024
Web site: http://www.fcpmc.com/home.asp
The FCPC is the national industry association represent-
ing the nation's food and consumer products industry. It
represents member companies ranging from small, inde-
pendently and privately owned companies to large global
multinationals, all of whom manufacture and distribute
food commodities in Canada.

National Futures Association (NFA)
300 South Riverside Plaza, #1800
Chicago, IL 60606
(312) 781-1300
Web site: http://www.nfa.org
The NFA is an industry-wide, self-regulatory organization.
It develops rules, programs, and services that safeguard
market integrity, protect investors, and help NFA members
meet their regulatory responsibilities.

U.S. Commodity Futures Trading Commission (CFTC)
Three Lafayette Centre
1155 21st Street NW

Washington, DC 20581
(202) 418-5000
Web site: http://www.cftc.gov
The CFTC encourages competitiveness and efficiency and
protects market participants against fraud and manipulation
by ensuring the financial integrity of the trading process.

WEB SITES

Due to the changing nature of Internet links, Rosen Publishing
has developed an online list of Web sites related to the subject
of this book. This site is updated regularly. Please use this link
to access the list:

http://www.rosenlinks.com/rwe/hctw

FOR FURTHER READING

Acton, Johnny, and David Goldblatt. *Economy*. New York,
    NY: DK, 2010.
Alexander, Colin. *Timing Techniques for Commodity
    Futures Markets: Effective Strategy and Tactics for
    Short-Term and Long-Term Traders*. New York, NY:
    McGraw-Hill, 2007.
Altman, Daniel. *Connected: 24 Hours in the Global Economy*.
    New York, NY: Picador, 2008.
Andrews, Carolyn. *What Are Goods and Services?* New York,
    NY: Crabtree Publishing Company, 2008.
Andrews, Carolyn. *What Is Trade?* New York, NY: Crabtree
    Publishing Company, 2008.
Brezina, Corona. *How Imports and Exports Work* (Real World
    Economics). New York, NY: Rosen Publishing, 2011.
Chicago Board of Trade. *The Chicago Board of Trade
    Handbook of Futures and Options*. New York, NY:
    McGraw-Hill, 2006.
Furgang, Kathy. *How the Stock Market Works* (Real World
    Economics). New York, NY: Rosen Publishing, 2010.
Griffis, Michael, and Lita Epstein. *Trading for Dummies*.
    Indianapolis, IN: For Dummies, 2009.
Hart, Joyce. *How Inflation Works* (Real World Economics).
    New York, NY: Rosen Publishing, 2009.

Holihan, Mary B. *The Complete Guide to Investing in Commodity Trading & Futures: How to Earn High Rates of Returns Safely.* Ocala, FL: Atlantic Publishing Group, 2008.

Hovey, Craig, with Gregory Rehmke. *The Complete Idiot's Guide to Global Economics.* Indianapolis, IN: Alpha Books, 2008.

Hudak, Heather C. *Spending* (Everyday Economics). New York, NY: Weigl Publishers, 2009.

Jankovsy, Jason Alan. *The Art of the Trade: What I Learned (and Lost) Trading the Chicago Futures Markets.* Hoboken, NJ: Wiley, 2008.

Merino, Noel. *The World Economy* (Current Controversies). San Diego, CA: Greenhaven Press, 2010.

Meyer, Susan. *How Buying and Selling Futures Works* (Real World Economics). New York, NY: Rosen Publishing, 2011.

Miller Debra A. *The U.S. Economy* (Current Controversies). San Diego, CA: Greenhaven Press, 2010.

Nagle, Jeanne. *How a Recession Works* (Real World Economics). New York, NY: Rosen Publishing, 2009.

Spurga, Ronald C. *Commodity Fundamentals: How to Trade the Precious Metals, Energy, Grain, and Tropical Commodity Markets.* Hoboken, NJ: Wiley, 2006.

Thompson, Gare. *What Is Supply and Demand?* New York, NY: Crabtree Publishing Company, 2009.

BIBLIOGRAPHY

AmericanEnergyIndependence.com. "Oil and the Iraq War." Retrieved February 2010 (http://www. americanenergyindependence.com/iraqwar.aspx).

Babcock, Bruce. "Commodity Futures Trading for Beginners." RB-Trading.com, 1999. Retrieved February 2010 (http://www.rb-trading.com/begin4.html).

Campbell, Elizabeth. "Florida Orange-Crop Forecast Rises on Freeze Review (Update 2)." *BusinessWeek*, March 10, 2010. Retrieved March 2010 (http://www. businessweek.com/news/2010-03-10/florida-orange-crop-estimate-increased-after-freeze-assessment.html).

Campbell, Elizabeth. "Orange Juice Extends Slump to Longest in Two Months on Forecast." *BusinessWeek*, March 10, 2010. Retrieved March 2010 (http://www.businessweek. com/news/2010-03-10/orange-juice-extends-slump-to-longest-in-two-months-on-forecast.html).

Chance, Don M. "Futures Market and Contracts." *Derivatives and Alternative Investments*. Boston, MA: Pearson Custom Publishing, 2009.

Commodity-TradingCompanies.com. "Playing the Commodities Boom." Retrieved February 2010 (http://commodity-tradingcompanies.com/playing-the-commodities-boom).

CommodityTrading.org. "What Do You Know About
    Trading Oil Commodities?" Retrieved February 2010
    (http://www.commodities-trading.org/commodities-
    trading-oil.html).

Dumon, Marv. "An Overview of Commodities Trading."
    Investopedia.com. Retrieved February 2010 (http://
    www.investopedia.com/articles/optioninvestor/09/
    commodity-trading.asp).

Guilford, Dave. "What Is a Commodity Broker?" eHow.
    com. Retrieved February 2010 (http://www.ehow.com/
    about_4672987_what-commodity-broker.html).

Holihan, Mary B. *The Complete Guide to Investing in Commodity
    Trading & Futures: How to Earn High Rates of Returns
    Safely.* Ocala, FL: Atlantic Publishing Group, 2008.

Indiviglio, Daniel. "How Traders Influence Prices." *The
    Atlantic,* September 11, 2009. Retrieved February
    2010 (http://business.theatlantic.com/2009/09/how_
    traders_influence_markets.php).

Jankovsy, Jason Alan. *The Art of the Trade: What I Learned
    (and Lost) Trading the Chicago Futures Markets.*
    Hoboken, NJ: Wiley, 2008.

Kolb, Robert W., and James A. Overdahl. *Futures, Options,
    and Swaps.* 5th ed. New York, NY: Blackwell
    Publishing, 2007.

Kowalski, Chuck. "Myths of Investing in Commodities." About.
    com. Retrieved February 2010 (http://commodities.
    about.com/od/gettingstarted/a/commoditiesmyth.htm).

Lehrich, Kelcey. "Commodities Trading Strategies." eHow.
    com. Retrieved February 2010 (http://www.ehow.com/
    way_5372957_commodities-trading-strategies.html).

McFerron, Whitney. "Cattle Prices May Rise as Exports Rebound, Doud Says." Bloomberg.com, January 27, 2010. Retrieved February 2010 (http://www.bloomberg.com/apps/news?pid=20601012&sid=a5IwH29D00sE).

Pendleton, Claudette. "How Does Commodity Trading Work?" eHow.com. Retrieved February 2010 (http://www.ehow.com/how-does_4689136_commodity-trading-work.html).

Spurga, Ronald C. *Commodity Fundamentals: How to Trade the Precious Metals, Energy, Grain, and Tropical Commodity Markets.* Hoboken, NJ: Wiley, 2006.

Sud, Hari. "China and India Driving World Metal Demand." UPIAsia.com. Retrieved February 2010 (http://www.upiasia.com/Economics/2008/04/08/china_and_india_driving_world_metal_demand/6087).

Tariq, Sohail. "Oil Is the Most Important Commodity at Present Time." SmasHits.com. Retrieved February 2010 (http://articles.smashits.com/articles/other/139417/oil-is-the-most-important-commodity-in-the-present-time.html).

Teo, Joel. "How to Make Money with Commodity Trading." EzineArticles.com. Retrieved February 2010 (http://ezinearticles.com/?How-To-Make-Money-With-Commodity-Trading&id=436168).

Whipps, Heather. "How Ancient Trade Changed the World." LiveScience.com, February 18, 2008. Retrieved February 2010 (http://www.livescience.com/history/080218-hs-trade.html).

Zakaria, Fareed. "Why We Can't Quit Oil." *Newsweek*, March 24, 2008. Retrieved February 2010 (http://www.newsweek.com/id/123482).

INDEX

About the Author

Laura La Bella is a writer and editor living in Rochester, New York. She has written numerous books on economics, natural resources, commodities, markets, and regulation, including *Not Enough to Drink: Pollution, Drought, and Tainted Water Supplies* and *Safety and the Food Supply*.

Photo Credits

Cover (top) © www.istockphoto.com/Lilli Day; cover (bottom), pp. 1 (right), 7, 19, 31, 43, 53, 60 Mario Tama/Getty Images; pp. 1 (left), 3, 4–5 © www.istockphoto.com/Dean Turner; p. 6 Matt Stroshane/Getty Images; p. 8–9 Peter Turner/Stone/Getty Images; p. 11 Spencer Platt/Getty Images; pp. 14–15 Willis D. Vaughn/National Geographic/Getty Images; pp. 16–17 Justin Sullivan/Getty Images; pp. 22–23 © CME Group, A CME/Chicago Board of Trade/NYMEX Company; p. 24 Scott Olson/Getty Images; pp. 26–27 Grey Villet/Time & Life Pictures/Getty Images; pp. 32–33 © AP Images; pp. 34–35, 48–49 Tim Boyle/Newsmakers/Getty Images; pp. 38–39 David Greedy/Getty Images; pp. 44–45 Jeff Haynes/Getty Images; p. 50 Francois Durand/Getty Images; p. 54 ChinaFotoPress/Getty Images; pp. 56, 61 Shutterstock; p. 58 Gary Gardiner/Bloomberg/Getty Images; p. 63 Jung Yeon-Je/AFP/Getty Images; p. 65 Ligia Botero/The Image Bank/Getty Images; pp. 68, 70, 73, 75, 78 © www.istockphoto.com/studiovision.

Photo Researcher: Marty Levick